Martha Washington

Martha Washington

By Joan F. Marsh

Franklin Watts

New York / Chicago / London / Sydney

A First Book

Washington

The quotations from Martha Washington's letters
are taken from copies in the library of the
Mount Vernon Ladies' Association.

Photographs copyright ©: Art Institute of Chicago, cover frame; Mount Vernon Ladies' Association, 2, 18, 19, 24, 25 (top & bottom), 35, (top left & right, bottom left), 39, 46, 55, 57, 59; Gibbes Museum of Art, Carolina Art Association, 10; Washington/Custis/Lee Collection, University, Lexington, Va., 15, 22, 35 (bottom right); North Wind Picture Archives, 16, 2l, 30 (top & bottom), 44, 58; The Carnegie Museum of Art, Howard Eavenson Americana Collection, 26; Lafayette College Art Collection, Easton, PA, 31; Yale University Art Gallery, Trumbull Collection, 36; The Metropolitan Museum of Art. Bequest of William Nelson, l905, 40; The New-York Historical Society, 45; Collection of the Newark Museum, bequest of Dr. J. Ackerman Coles, 1926, 47; National Portrait Gallery, Washington, D.C./Art Resources, NY, 48; The Historical Society of Pennsylvania, 51.

Library of Congress Cataloging-in-Publication Data
Martha Washington / by Joan F. Marsh.
p. cm.—(A First book)
Includes bibliographical references and index.
Summary: A biography of America's first first lady.
ISBN 0-531-20145-7 (HC lib. bdg.)
1. Washington, Martha, 1731–1802—Juvenile literature.
2. Washington, George, 1732–1799—Juvenile literature.
3. Presidents—United States—Wives—Biography—Juvenile literature. [1. Washington, Martha, 1731–1802. 2. First ladies.] I. Title. II. Series.
E312.19.W34M37 1993
973.4'1'092—dc20[B]
92-24531 CIP AC

For Alex, Jeff, Ned, Dash,
Emma, and Franca

★　★　★　★　★

Contents

★ ★ ★ ★ ★

★　★　★　★　★

ACKNOWLEDGMENTS

The author wishes to express her appreciation for
the courteous assistance of the library staff of the
Mount Vernon Ladies' Association.
Special thanks go to John Riley, Archivist,
for reviewing the manuscript.

★ ★ ★ ★ ★

CHAPTER ONE

A
Virginia Girl

★ ★ ★ ★ ★

*L*ess than one hundred years before Martha Washington was born, the colony of Virginia was the homeland of Indian chiefs and their people. But a great tide of settlers from England arrived who took their land and cleared the forests for their plantations. Soon the Indian hunters were gone. Settlers and their families lined the bays and rivers near their new capital of Williamsburg.

John Dandridge was a tobacco planter like his neighbors. He built a large frame house on the

*Large plantations had rows of small cabins, called
"The Quarters," for their slaves to live in.*

Pamunkey River for his new wife, Frances. It was called Chestnut Grove. On the second of June 1731, their first child was born. They named her Martha, after her grandmother.

Soon Martha had several brothers and sisters. They played with tops and dolls, and there were always enough people for hopscotch or tag. But in between games Martha had many serious tasks. While she was still quite small her mother showed her how to knit stockings and mittens for the family. Many hours were spent practicing neat embroidery stitches, too. While her brothers were off with their guns or their horses, Martha would be at her mother's side helping her to cure a ham or whip the eggs for a special cake.

Parents in Martha's day didn't think that a girl needed to have much regular schooling. It was enough for her to learn to read, write, and do simple arithmetic. The most important thing was for her to grow up to be a good wife and mother.

By the time she was fifteen, Martha had matured into a graceful young lady. She was small, like all the Dandridge women, barely five feet tall. Her soft brown hair was gathered away from her face, setting off her dark hazel eyes. She had learned country dances and minutes, and she could play a lively tune on the spinet. She was ready to be introduced to polite society.

Soon she was being asked to parties with her mother and father. When they went to Williamsburg, she was invited to balls at the Governor's Palace. It was not long before she captured the heart of the most eligible bachelor in the Pamunkey Valley.

Daniel Parke Custis was twenty years older than Martha, but he was handsome and kind. The Custises were members of a wealthy and distinguished family. They owned thousands of acres of land, and many black slaves. Everyone thought she was a lucky girl to have made such a fine match.

In 1749, when she was eighteen years old, Martha and Daniel Custis were married at Chestnut Grove. Then they went to live at Daniel's plantation, just up the river. By an odd twist of fate, her new home was called the White House.

Martha and Daniel had four children: Daniel, Frances, John (Jacky), and Martha (Patsy). But tragedy soon struck their family. First little Daniel died, and then Frances. In the summer of 1757, Martha's husband, too, died of a sudden illness.

It was a sad time for Martha, but she was determined to be independent. For the next year and a half, the young widow managed her husband's estates. Because the property was too vast to oversee herself, she had a steward to help her. But Martha was the one who checked the shipments of tobacco and wrote the English merchants about the price she expected in return.

Only twenty-six years old, Martha Custis was one of the wealthiest and most attractive widows in the colony. She knew that she must marry again, and quickly. She needed help in managing her inheritance and raising her children. But she must find a man who would be a good father for Jacky and Patsy, and who was not just interested in her fortune.

CHAPTER TWO

Mount Vernon

★ ★ ★ ★ ★

*E*arly in the spring of 1758, Martha's neighbors, the Chamberlaynes, invited her to dinner. Just as they were about to sit down, Richard Chamberlayne came in with another guest. He was a tall handsome gentleman in the uniform of a colonel in the Virginia Regiment. He seemed quite shy, but his grey-blue eyes were direct as they looked into hers. She recognized him right away. It was George Washington, hero of a famous battle on the frontier. He could only just stay for dinner, he said. He was carrying important

George Washington in the uniform of the Virginia Regiment, which he wore during the French and Indian War. This picture was painted by Charles Willson Peale in 1772.

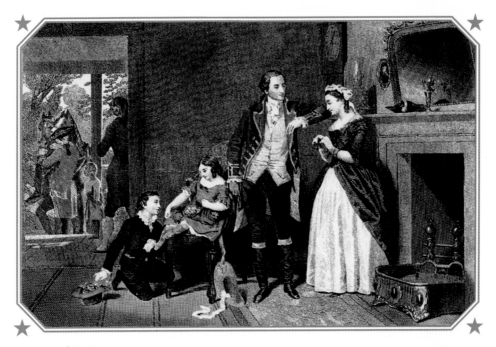

George Washington visited Martha at the White House soon after they met at the Chamberlayes. Some people think that he asked her to marry him on this visit.

papers for the Governor in Williamsburg. But the sun began to set, and George Washington was still there. He didn't want to leave the charming widow.

It was only a short time later that George asked Martha to marry him. He was going to resign from the army and become a planter. They decided to be married at the White House on Saturday, January 6, 1759.

Martha and George made a handsome couple on their wedding day. Martha wore a dress of rich yellow brocade over a petticoat quilted with silver thread. Her satin shoes had high heels, but still her brown head only came up to her husband's shoulder.

In the spring, the Washingtons moved to George's plantation, Mount Vernon. Martha and the children were anxious to see their new home. It was a white frame house with big chimneys at either end. The second story had just been added to make room for them. When Martha walked through the big hall and out onto the lawn, she saw the wide Potomac River sparking below. It was beautiful. She knew at once why George loved Mount Vernon so much.

The next months were busy ones for the young couple. The farms had been neglected while George was in the army. Fences needed mending and barns must be built. Martha organized the house and helped to choose some new furnishings to be ordered from London.

She found that her husband liked a strict routine. They were both up at dawn. After a breakfast of corn-cakes and honey, George rode out to inspect the plantation. Martha always spent a quiet hour reading her Bible. Then she was ready for the day.

First she crossed over to the kitchen with its huge open fireplace. It was in one of the small buildings that were clustered about the courtyard. With Doll, the cook, Martha planned the meals for the household. Dinner was served promptly at three in the afternoon. It

Mount Vernon in 1792, showing the large piazza, or porch, overlooking the river. When Martha first saw the house it was quite a bit smaller than it is in this picture.

was not easy to know how many people would be there. In addition to the family and invited guests, no traveler or visitor would be turned away.

With dinner under way, Martha could see to her other duties. Once a week Jenny washed and Mima ironed mountains of laundry under her supervision. Sewing and mending were a daily chore. Later she might stop by the slave quarters to give an ailing servant herbs from her medicine chest. If there was time before dinner, Martha could be found in the gardens she loved.

This view of Mount Vernon shows a family on the bowling green in front of the house.

When George came back from his rounds of the plantation, Martha was clean and cool, making their guests feel at home. She must have been lonely at first, in spite of the lively household. Her old home was many miles away. But in her easy way, she soon made her husband's friends her own.

In one of his letters George wrote of the happiness that his new family had brought him. He wanted nothing more, he said, than to spend the rest of his life with Martha at Mount Vernon.

CHAPTER THREE

The Darkening Sky

★ ★ ★ ★ ★

For some years life continued in this peaceful pattern for Martha and her husband. George became a leader in their community. He was elected to represent their county in the government of the colony, too. When he traveled to Williamsburg, Martha and the children often went with him. They stayed with her sister Nancy, who lived at Eltham plantation nearby.

No new babies joined the family at Mount Vernon, but George came to love Patsy and Jacky as if they

John Parke (Jacky) Custis and Martha Parke (Patsy) Custis, painted by John Wollaston. As you can see, children at this time were dressed as if they were small adults.

were his own. Dark-haired Patsy was his special pet. She was a frail, gentle girl. By the time she was twelve, George and Martha knew that she had epilepsy. There were no drugs then to treat this disease. Martha took her to many doctors in search of a cure. As she grew older, the frightening seizures increased.

Fortunately, Jacky was in the pink of health. Martha adored him and closed her eyes to his faults. He was a handsome, impulsive boy, and he hated school. He did poorly in mathematics and badly at languages. To tell the truth, he didn't even spell very well. He liked to be outdoors with his horse and his gun.

George was determined that Jacky should have a good education. He sent him to college in New York, but Jacky had other things on his mind. He had fallen in love with pretty Eleanor (Nelly) Calvert from Maryland. When he was nineteen, Jacky left college to marry Nelly. George went with him to Maryland for the wedding. Martha stayed home, for she was in mourning. Patsy had died during one of her seizures.

On December 16, 1773, just before Jacky's wedding, something happened in Massachusetts that was going to change all their lives. A group of men disguised as Indians threw a cargo of tea into Boston Harbor. They called it a "Boston Tea Party." They were protesting the taxes that England had put on the tea.

(Above) *A* chair cushion stitched by Martha. She made twelve of these cushions, and it took her thirty-six years to finish them all.

(Opposite, top) Martha Washington's satin wedding shoes.

(Opposite, bottom) Some of the simple jewelry that Martha preferred. All the things on these two pages are in the museum at Mount Vernon.

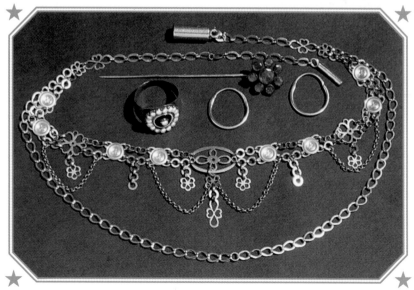

Amos Doolittle, a Connecticut militiaman, engraved this scene of the Battle of Lexington.

None of the colonists liked being taxed by the English Parliament. They called a Congress in Philadelphia to decide what to do. Washington was elected as a delegate from Virginia. Martha sent him off with a troubled heart and a smiling face. "I hope you will all stand firm," she said to his companions. "I know George will." At Philadelphia the delegates agreed not to trade goods with England until the colonies were treated more fairly.

It was not long before more trouble broke out. British troops searching for ammunition in Massachusetts clashed with Americans in Lexington and Concord. New England colonists had formed an army of farmers, with no one to lead them.

A second Continental Congress was called in 1775. This time Martha took George's old uniform out of the trunk where it had lain since he resigned from the Virginia Regiment. The Congress chose him to be the Commander in Chief of the new Continental Army.

The American Revolution had begun.

CHAPTER FOUR

A
General's Wife

★ ★ ★ ★ ★

When Washington took command of the Continental Army, he worried about leaving Martha alone. He was afraid that she was in danger. The British thought that the rebels were traitors. If the Revolution failed, their property would be taken away from them. Their leaders would be harshly punished. Martha could be taken hostage by the British army. She would be a valuable tool to force the colonists to surrender.

After Washington joined the army in Massachusetts, there was a rumor that the royal governor of Virginia was going to take Martha prisoner and burn

Mount Vernon. She packed up Washington's papers and some of their valuables in a trunk, so that they could be moved in a hurry. Then she went to stay with Nancy at Eltham.

While she was there, she got a letter from her husband. He invited her to join him at his headquarters in Cambridge, Massachusetts, outside of Boston. Martha had never traveled farther than Williamsburg or nearby Annapolis, Maryland. The trip would take almost a month. The roads would be icy and rutted with the coming winter weather. Martha did not hesitate. By the middle of November she was in the big Mount Vernon coach on her way to Cambridge.

Everyone thought that the war would be over quickly. But Martha spent eight years in winter camps with her husband. Later she claimed that she heard the first gun and the last one of every campaign of the Revolution. In the spring, when the armies began to move, she returned home to Mount Vernon. There she coped with wartime fears and shortages, and waited for yet another summons to camp in the north.

Each year Washington chose a place for his winter headquarters where he could watch the movements of the enemy. Cambridge, Morristown, Valley Forge, Middlebrook, New Windsor, Newburgh—his camps followed the tide of the war as it shifted up and down the coast from New England to Pennsylvania.

(Above) *Washington's headquarters in Newburgh, New York, where Martha and her husband spent the last year of the Revolutionary War. The small Dutch farmhouse overlooks the Hudson River.*

(Left) *The headquarters had an unusual fireplace, which has no sides and no mantel. A small fire was lit in the middle of the hearth.*

Martha was soon joined by other officers' wives. They tried to make Headquarters more homelike for their husbands. Martha was deeply concerned about the men of the rank and file of the army too. At Valley Forge, in the winter of 1778, conditions were particularly harsh. The Continental Army had lost some heartbreaking battles. Many of the men were barefoot in the winter snow. They were short of food as well. Martha did what she could to help them. The soldiers loved her, and called her "Lady Washington."

George Washington visiting the suffering soldiers at Valley Forge.

One of the young girls in the neighborhood sometimes went with her when she visited the men. This is what she said:

> I never in my life knew a woman so busy from early morning until late at night as was Lady Washington, providing comforts for the sick soldiers. Everyday, excepting Sundays, the wives of officers in camp, and sometimes other women, were invited. . . . to assist her in knitting socks, patching garments, and making shirts for the poor soldiers when materials could be procured. Every fair day she might be seen, with basket in hand, and with a single attendant, going among the huts seeking the keenest and most needy sufferers, and giving all the comfort to them in her power.

After this dark and terrible winter, the Americans received good news from Europe. The French had entered the war as their allies. They were sending troops and ships to help them in their struggle against the British.

CHAPTER FIVE

The
Long Road to Peace

★ ★ ★ ★ ★

For three more years, the war dragged on. Then one day in September 1781, Washington cantered up to the door of Mount Vernon. He had not been home for more than six years. He was on his way to Yorktown, Virginia, where a large British army was camped. The Americans and their French allies had marched all the way from New York to fight them.

For two days the house was crowded with French and American officers. Spurs jingled in the hall and heavy boots rang on the stairs. It sounded just like winter camp. Everyone was talking about the battle to come. Jacky listened eagerly. He had spent the war watching out for his mother and taking care of his growing family. Now he could tell that victory was near. He wanted to be part of it. When Washington galloped to Yorktown with his officers, a proud Jacky was with him. He had volunteered to be an aide to his stepfather.

Martha and Nelly waited anxiously for news of the battle. The Americans had laid siege to the British fortifications. For days, their cannons pounded the little town. Finally, on the 19th of October, the enemy surrendered. It was a great victory, but their joy soon turned to sorrow. Jacky had come down with "camp fever," and was desperately ill. Martha and Nelly hurried to his side. Several days later Jacky died.

Nelly was left with three little daughters and a baby son to care for. Martha well understood the situation that Nelly was in. Martha and George would help her as much as they could. Perhaps some of the children could come to stay at Mount Vernon.

But the war was not over yet, and Washington had to be with his troops. When he left for his headquarters at Newburgh, New York, Martha was with him. The next two years were difficult ones. Everyone knew that the Americans had won the war, but a peace treaty had not been signed. The army was idle and restless at the camp on the Hudson River.

Eliza Parke Custis; Martha (Patty) Parke Custis; Eleanor (Nelly) Parke Custis; George Washington (Little Washington) Parke Custis. These portraits were painted by artist Robert Edge Pine in 1785.

Washington resigning his commission as commander-in-chief of the Continental Army. The artist has painted Martha in the balcony, but actually she was at home waiting for George to come home for Christmas dinner.

Martha had been a good soldier throughout the long war. Now she too was feeling the strain. During the summer of 1783, she was ill with a high fever. When George was ready to leave camp, she was too sick to travel. Weeks later she was still weak and tired. In October, she went home to Mount Vernon at last. A treaty had been signed, and George promised to be home for Christmas dinner.

On Christmas Eve, the door was flung wide to welcome him. In his bags were presents for everyone. A locket and a dress cap for Martha, and a new silver coffee pot with the family crest. There was a whirligig and a fiddle and a toy gun for his grandson. The little girls had pocketbooks, thimbles, and sashes.

Peace had come to Mount Vernon.

CHAPTER SIX

A
Convention Called

★ ★ ★ ★ ★

$\mathcal{A}$s the new year began,
Martha wrote to a friend: "My little family are all with
me, and have been very well till with in these few days,
that they have been taken with the measles. The worst I
hope is over, and that I shall soon have them prattling
about me again. . . ."

Two of Martha's grandchildren had come to
make their home at Mount Vernon. Eleanor Parke
Custis (called Nelly by the family), was already a beauty
at five years old. Her brother George Washington Parke

Fanny Bassett, Martha's favorite niece, was also painted by artist Robert Edge Pine.

Lafayette visiting the Washingtons at Mount Vernon after the Revolutionary War. The artists show them standing on the piazza overlooking the river.

Custis, aged three, was so round and plump that they nicknamed him "Tub." It was wonderful to have children in the house again. Soon another young person joined the family. Fanny Bassett was the daughter of Martha's sister Nancy. Her mother had died, and Martha persuaded her father to let Fanny come to Mount Vernon too.

It was a crowded household, for the Washingtons always had guests. All kinds of people came to see the famous Revolutionary hero. George himself compared his house to a "well-resorted tavern, as scarcely any strangers who are going from north to south, or from south to north, do not spend a day or two at it."

They had many distinguished visitors as well. One of Martha's favorites was a young Frenchman, Marie Joseph Paul Yves Roche Gilbert du Motier, the Marquis de Lafayette. He had volunteered to join Washington's staff during the war, and had grown to be almost like a son to him. Martha didn't pay any attention to his title. She called him "the French boy." Artists, too, came to make portraits of her husband. One of them, Robert Edge Pine, stayed for three weeks and painted pictures of all the grandchildren.

Because of their many guests, Washington had decided to enlarge the house again. Much of the work had been planned before the Revolution. Now the additions were almost finished. On the north end of the house was a big, two-story dining room with plenty of space for dining or dancing. The south wing had a study for George. Above it was their new bedroom, which was separated from the busy central part of the house. It gave Martha a quiet place for her letter writing and her religious devotions.

By 1787, Washington was already being drawn into national affairs again. The government of the young republic was not a strong one. It was really just an agreement by the states that they wanted to work together. People were already saying that they wanted to divide into smaller nations, or find a king who could bring order to the country. A convention was called to deal with the crisis. Again, George represented Virginia.

The Constitutional Convention that met in Philadelphia saw that a whole new government was needed. It should have a congress to represent the people and courts to interpret the laws. A president would direct the government. Only one man seemed to be the right choice for president: George Washington.

George did not want to be in public life again. He and Martha loved their tranquil country life. But on April 14, 1789, the Secretary of the Congress came to Mount Vernon with important news. Washington had been unanimously elected as the first president of the United States.

CHAPTER SEVEN

The First First Lady

★ ★ ★ ★ ★

New York was the capital of the new republic. Washington left right away to attend the inauguration ceremonies at Federal Hall. Martha came as soon as she could, bringing Nelly and little Washington. Fanny stayed behind to help take care of Mount Vernon. Martha was surprised to find crowds lining the streets to cheer her in the cities along the way. "Dear little Washington," she wrote Fanny, "seemed to be lost in a maze at the great parade that was made for us all the way that we came."

*Thousands of people came to see their new
president arrive in New York, and cannons were
fired to salute him.*

New York was a crowded, bustling city.

The children found the city very exciting; Martha reported that Nelly spent hours at the window, watching the carriages pass in the crowded streets. For herself, though, it was a difficult change from their life at Mount Vernon. She soon discovered that her time was not her own. She was no longer a private person, but the wife of the first president.

*Artist Jennie Brownscombe painted this
scene of a special ball given by the
Washingtons. She has made Martha look
much taller than she actually was.*

Everyone wanted to meet them. George received gentlemen callers on Tuesday afternoons. Martha entertained the ladies and their husbands on Friday evenings. Sometimes the elegantly dressed guests would linger too long. Then Martha would rise and say gently, "The General always retires at nine, and I usually precede him."

On Thursdays they invited special guests to dinner. The long table was set in the latest French fashion. Their steward was in charge of everything. He was the famous "Black Sam Fraunces," who owned a tavern in New York. He prepared all kinds of delicacies, including that wonderful new dessert, ice cream. Martha enjoyed these parties, for many members of the government were friends from Revolutionary days.

As time went by, life became more pleasant for Martha. She went for drives in the carriage, behind the matched bay horses that were her husband's pride. She took Nelly and little Washington to visit the waxworks to see the statute of George in his Revolutionary uniform. She had part of the attic made into a playroom for the children, where they liked to stage plays for their grandmother. She made new friends, such as Abigail Adams, wife of the vice president.

They had only been in New York a little more than a year when they had to move again. Congress had

Edward Savage completed this portrait of the first family in 1796. Martha is pointing to a map of the new "Capital City" being build on the Potomac River. Nelly stands by her, and Little Washington is standing where his grandfather can keep an eye on him.

voted to establish a new federal city on the Potomac River, near the center of the Republic. It would be called Washington, in honor of the first president. While it was being built, the seat of the government would be at Philadelphia.

Their friends, the Robert Morrises, had agreed to rent them their beautiful mansion on High Street. Plans were being made to enlarge the house for the president. In the meantime, they would go home to Mount Vernon for the first time since Washington took office. They had hoped that no ceremony would be planned for their departure, but all the local dignitaries came to escort them to the dock. Cannon salutes thundered over the harbor as they left New York.

CHAPTER EIGHT

Philadelphia

★ ★ ★ ★ ★

*I*n November 1790, Martha and her family moved into the Morris house in Philadelphia. Hammers were still banging in the background. The smell of paint hung in the air. An addition had been built for the servants, and the stables had been made larger for the presidential horses. George's office was on the third floor, and his secretaries slept two to a room nearby. Every corner of the big house was filled.

The new capital was a lively, prosperous place. Ships from all over the world pulled up to the docks on Front Street. The city had a library, a philosophical soci-

*Philadelphia from across the Delaware River.
The Washington's house was on High Street.*

ety, and a museum where stuffed birds and animals could be seen. Philadelphians were known for their gaiety, too. They had picnics, dances, and assembly balls.

Martha had visited the city often during the Revolution. She had many good friends there. On Christmas Eve, they had a reception, and she wore a new black velvet dress. She was enjoying herself and getting about more than she had in New York. She took the carriage for visits to country estates and shopped for presents to send to Fanny and the others at home. Her evening receptions were more popular than ever. From time to time she went to the theater with George.

The children liked Philadelphia, too. Nelly took dancing lessons and was learning to play the harpsichord. Many hours were spent practicing under her grandmother's watchful eye. Nine-year-old Little Washington was going to the Philadelphia Academy.

In 1793, Washington was unanimously reelected as president for a second term. He had wanted to retire, but his advisors persuaded him to run again. They said that the Republic would be in danger without his impartial leadership. It was true that the country seemed to be splitting into factions. The bankers and merchants of the north were led by Alexander Hamilton. Thomas Jefferson spoke for the farmers in the south. Opposing newspapers fed the flames.

It was hard for Martha to read the articles criticizing her husband. She knew that the people still loved their president. But his second term was plagued by problems. Many people opposed the new treaty that was signed with England. Relations with France were strained. Frontiersmen in Pennsylvania refused to pay taxes on the whiskey they made. Washington had to lead government troops to quell the "Whiskey Rebellion."

When the time came to consider yet another term, Washington stood firm. Another man should take the helm. Martha could not help but be glad. She had done her best as the first first lady, but she always referred to the presidency as her "lost days." She and George were in their mid-sixties now. Mount Vernon had been neglected while they were away. It was time to go home.

The campaign of 1796 was an exciting one. It was the nation's first contested election. Vice President John Adams ran against Thomas Jefferson. When the ballots were counted, Adams had won by only two votes.

On February 22, 1797, Washington's birthday was celebrated with a general holiday. Schools were dismissed, and servants were given the day off. The big arena at Rickett's Circus was packed to the rafters for the ball in his honor. Hundreds of people came to say farewell to their beloved president and his first lady.

The first week in March, John Adams was inaugurated president of the United States. Washington walked alone to the ceremony at Congress Hall. He was calm and serene. Like Martha, he had no regrets at leaving public life.

CHAPTER NINE

Home to Mount Vernon

★ ★ ★ ★ ★

A few days after the inauguration, George and Martha were on their way to Mount Vernon. Martha and Nelly rode in the coach. Behind it rolled the wagons with the servants and the baggage. In one of them the family dog barked and the family parrot cackled. At the last moment, Martha inquired anxiously about the Italian myrtle for her garden. Shipped by water were ninety-seven boxes, fourteen trunks, thirteen packages, three hampers and other odds and ends.

Martha wasn't feeling well. She had a bad cold. It gave them an excuse to avoid some of the ceremonies that had been planned for them along the way. Even so they were greeted by huge crowds in Baltimore, and a military escort led them through the new federal city. A crowd of people met them at the ferry landing in Alexandria, and rode with them all the way to Mount Vernon.

It took quite a while to get everything unpacked. They had brought home with them some furniture from the presidential mansion. The big comfortable bed that

Martha's desk, in her bedroom at Mount Vernon. This was her "command post" for directing the activities of the plantation. Her basket of keys sits on top of the desk.

had been made for them in Philadelphia went into their bedroom. Nelly's harpsichord fitted nicely in the little parlor.

They soon settled into their old routine, but many changes had taken place during the eight years they were gone. Hardest for Martha was the loss of Fanny, who had died the year before. Nelly's older sisters, Eliza and Martha, were both married now, with children of their own. They lived in the federal city and often drove out for visits.

Not even Nelly seemed to miss the gay life of the capital. She was now a beautiful young lady of eighteen, with several suitors. One of them was Lawrence Lewis, Washington's nephew. George had asked him to come to Mount Vernon to help them with their many guests. He was handsome and tall, and people said that he looked like his uncle.

Washington Custis had entered college in New Jersey. He was growing up to be as carefree and undisciplined as his father had been. He soon got into some kind of trouble and came home again. His grandfather wrote him out a strict schedule for studying, but he couldn't seem to stick to it. Like Jacky, he was happiest outdoors with his gun on his shoulder.

Just before Christmas 1798, Nelly and Lawrence surprised everyone at Mount Vernon by becoming engaged. They wanted to be married on Washington's birthday. On February 22, all the candles in the big house were lit. George put on his Revolutionary blue and buff uniform once again and gave the bride away. The young couple decided to make their home at Mount Vernon after their marriage. Before long, a baby was on the way. In November 1799, Nelly had a little girl. They named her Frances Parke Lewis and tucked her into the pretty crib that Martha had given them.

The Nelly Custis bedroom at Mount Vernon, with the crib given to Nelly by Martha.

One morning shortly after the baby was born Washington set out on his daily rounds of the plantation. The weather was cold and rainy. The next day he woke up with a sore throat. Before long he was very ill. Late on the night of the 14th of December he died.

After his death Martha closed the bedroom that they had shared for so many years. She moved to a small, plain room on the third floor. She had a fire for warmth, a narrow bed, and a chair or two for company. It was all she needed. One thing was on her mind. Her letters from George. She didn't want others reading them after she was gone. She decided to destroy them. Perhaps she

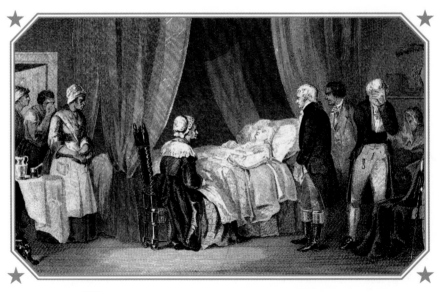

Martha sat at the foot of his bed during the long night when Washington died.

The little room where Martha slept during her last years.

put the bundles into the fire. Only two letters survive. They were found in a corner of her desk by one of her granddaughters.

Although Nelly and Lawrence were building a house of their own, they stayed on at Mount Vernon to keep an eye on her. Washington Custis slept in the bedroom right across the hall, too. Martha still came down every day to visit with their guests, but little Frances was her favorite companion. And so she lived quietly until the spring of 1802. When she became ill in May, the doctors did their best, but Martha was ready. She was going to join her beloved friend, George Washington.

Custis, George Washington Parke. *Private Memoirs of Washington*. Philadelphia: Edgewood Publishing Company, 1859.

Decatur, Stephen, Jr. *Private Affairs of George Washington*. Boston: Houghton Mifflin Company, 1933.

Fitzpatrick, John C., ed. *The Writings of George Washington* 39 Vols. Washington, DC: U.S. Printing Office, 1931–1944.

Flexnor, James Thomas. *George Washington*. 4 vols. Boston: Little, Brown and Company, 1965–1972.

Freeman, Douglas Southall. *George Washington: A Biography*. 7 vols. New York: Charles Scribner's Sons, 1948–1957.

Longworth, Polly "Portrait of Martha, Belle of New Kent," printed in *Colonial Williamsburg: the Journal of the Colonial Williamsburg Foundation*, Summer, 1988.

Lossing, Benson J. *Mary and Martha, The Mother and Wife of Washington* New York: Harper and Brothers, 1886.

Mount Vernon, A Handbook. Mount Vernon, VA: The Mount Vernon Ladies' Association, 1985

Thane, Elswyth. *Washington's Lady.* New York: Dodd, Mead and Company, 1960.

___. *Potomac Squire.* Mount Vernon, VA: Mount Vernon Ladies' Association, 1963.

Wall, Charles Cecil. *George Washington, Citizen Soldier.* Charlottesville: University Press of Virginia, 1980.

Wharton, Anne Hollingsworth. *Martha Washington.* New York: Charles Scribner's Sons, 1897.

Index

About the Author

*J*oan Marsh was inspired to write *Martha Washington* by her admiration for the subject and her feeling that "the first lady is rarely undersood as the charming and courageous woman that she was." Much of the research for this book took place at the Mount Vernon library, as well as many of the actual historical sites described in the book, including Martha Washington's birthplace, the headquarters where she stayed during the Revolution, and the area of Philadelphia where she lived during George Washington's presidency.

In addition to this First Book biography, Mrs. Marsh researched and wrote scripts for three educational video tapes on Maryland history: *17th Century Maryland, Its History and Its People, 18th Century Maryland*, and *Aaron's Story*.

The author lives in Chevy Chase, Maryland with her husband, Richard; they have four children and six grandchildren.